THY *Ways* ARE DIFFERENT

COLLETTE NLEMCHI

BALBOA.PRESS
A DIVISION OF HAY HOUSE

Scripture quotations marked KJV are from the Holy Bible, King James Version
(Authorized Version). First published in 1611. Quoted from the KJV Classic
Reference Bible, Copyright © 1983 by The Zondervan Corporation.

Balboa Press books may be ordered through booksellers or by contacting:

Balboa Press
A Division of Hay House
1663 Liberty Drive
Bloomington, IN 47403
www.balboapress.com
844-682-1282

Because of the dynamic nature of the Internet, any web addresses or
links contained in this book may have changed since publication and
may no longer be valid. The views expressed in this work are solely those
of the author and do not necessarily reflect the views of the publisher,
and the publisher hereby disclaims any responsibility for them.

The author of this book does not dispense medical advice or prescribe the use
of any technique as a form of treatment for physical, emotional, or medical
problems without the advice of a physician, either directly or indirectly. The
intent of the author is only to offer information of a general nature to help
you in your quest for emotional and spiritual well-being. In the event you use
any of the information in this book for yourself, which is your constitutional
right, the author and the publisher assume no responsibility for your actions.

Any people depicted in stock imagery provided by Getty Images are
models, and such images are being used for illustrative purposes only.
Certain stock imagery © Getty Images.

Print information available on the last page.

ISBN: 978-1-9822-5133-8 (sc)
ISBN: 978-1-9822-5134-5 (e)

Balboa Press rev. date: 08/06/2020

CONTENTS

1. YOUR WAYS ARE DIFFERENT

Oh! Glorious One, Heaven and Earth Adore thee.
None is like thee and none can be compared with thee.
Thou who made Heaven and Earth.
You, the unfathomable Sea.
The Wonderful and Powerful Deity
On my Knees I Bow Down.

Mankind is full of ignorance.
And thou sees everything.
Sometimes, Mankind wonders and ask why?
Because, they lack Wisdom and Perfection.

Your ways Oh! Heaven is Different.
Mankind Proposes and Heaven Disposes.
Because, it is not the write way.
Thou art the King of the Universe.
Everybody is under your Command.
And it is all about what you want.
Blessed and Glory be unto you, OH! Heaven.

Evangelist Collette Nlemchi 7/11/2018

2. I HAVE SEEN IT ALL

I have seen it all.
I have seen it all.
The Darkness and the Light.
The Good and the Bad.
The Wicked and the Pure.
Heaven Judges them all.

Taket not matters unto thy hands.
Because thou shall hurt thyself.
Put your trust and Battle unto him.
And thou shall free thyself.

What, and Who can you fight?
He is the one who is the greatest.
And he fights the battle for thee.
He made Heavens and Earth.
And He has the greatest Ammunition.

Collette Nlemchi 7/11/2018

3. WORRY NOT ABOUT THE FLASHINESS

The meek, Lowly, and Righteous,
The Heavens belongs to you.
Worry not about the Flashiness.
Very soon, thou shall see the prince of Peace.

His perfection is beyond all humans.
He comes in different Colors, Forms, Shapes and Sizes.
He is in disguise and No Man can Tell.
He giveth and taketh according to his will.

Collette Nlemchi 7/11/2018

4. ENDLESS IS HIS NAME

Oh! Thou who created the World.
No Mountain is bigger than thee.
No Jupiter thou cannot crush.
The chosen ones look unto thee.
Because they are Bold.
Thou protect the chosen ones who look unto thee.
Thou destroys the scheme of the Enemies.
Unto Eternal Fire they shall Burn.

Powerful and Mighty One,
Thou knoweth everything hidden under the Sun.
The evil People and their evil thou knoweth.
For the Hail Stones you send, they shall not escape.
The Wind will bear Witness.
The Rain drops will testify.
How wonderful and powerful thou art.

　　Collette Nlemchi 7/18/18

5. THE MIND

The Mind, thou who traveleth like the rapidity of a machine gun.
Thou can create and Thou can Destroy.
Thou can Pray and thou can move Mountains.

Thou Commandeth the Wonders.
Thou art equipped and Powerful.
When I read the Bible Verses.
I found out, thou art indeed Wonderful.
The things you do and the powers you Possess.

Oh! Mind, thou art in constant touch with Revelation.
Thou also giveth Redemption.
Let not your Mind imagine vain Things.
Look unto Heaven and thou shall imagine things of Great Price.
Imagine Greatness and thou shall Possess.

Collette Nlemchi. 7/18/18

6. UNPREDICTABLE LIFE

Oh! Life thou art very unpredictable.
Thou bringeth Misery to the World.
There are Cries all over the Universe.
Thou also bringeth Joy Unspeakable.

Thou art the only one who controls the Universe.
You take Away that which you have given.
Man's wants are Insatiable. Non is Satisfied.
Is only the grace that gives Satisfaction.
And thy Ways are different from our Ways.

Thou bringeth Misery and thou bringeth Joy.
It is only You who Consolate the Mind.
It is only thou who giveth and Taket.
Some things are beyond Human Understanding.

The Heavens, The Stars, The Moon, Thou Market them all.
The Most Powerful Creature is afraid of You.
This is because None is Like Thee.
Oh! Heaven Thou Shall have Mercy on those Under Your umbrella.

Collette Nlemchi 9/1/2018

7. FOOLS ARE THOU

It is only the Fools who say there is no greater power.
Oh! Greatest Power, Have Mercy and Direct My Foot Steps.
Because I believe in YOU.

Thou Bringeth Forth Powerful Cherubis All Around us.
Thou Protect Us From Harmful Creatures.
Jelous and Satanic Creatures that Roam Around The World.
Forces Of Darkness are Defeated By the Angels Of Light.

Collette Nlemchi. 9/1/18

8. TIME FOR GREATNESS

It is time for greatness.
What can I do Now?
For the whole World Revolves.
And the Hollies are Praying.
Also Singing Songs Of Joy.

We are all Sojourners on Earth.
Trying To Please the Biggest.
He do appreciate Our Endeavors.
To Make The World a Better Place.

Put Your Trust in Him.
For He Never Fail.
Oh! Universe, Where are You?
I am Under Your Umbrella.
And I will do What You Want Me To Do.

Collette Nlemchi. 3/2018

9. I HAVE SEEN THE LIGHT

I have seen the Light.
The Light that shines above the Sky.
The Light becomes Day.
And when Dark, It is Night.

Oh! Mystery, what can I say?
Your Creation and Invention Baffles Me.
The Beauties of Your Creation Makes Me To Wonder.
On My Knees I Bow Down For You.
For Thou Art Indeed The Greatest.

3/2018. Collette Nlemchi

10. THE WORLD ADORE THEE

The whole world adore thee.
Heaven and Earth are happy for you.
The birds of the Air Sings for Joy.
There is nothing like you in the Universe.
YOU, THE UNFATHOMABLE SEA.

I Adore thee Oh! Greatest One.
I bow down for You.
Praising you all the days of my life.
Thou who giveth and taketh.
The Holy One Of Isreal.
    You came in a Disguise.
And Mankind Did Not Know.
Wonders and Miracles You Performed.
And You Astonished Humanity by Your Actions.

On The Third Day, You Broke The Ground.
Showing Those Fools You Are Powerful.
You Mysteriously Showed Yourself again.
For Those who doubt should know.
Thou art the power of all Powers.

3/20/18 Collette Nlemchi

11. MASTER DESIGNER

Master designer I call you.
From the beginning you design the Universe.
The Heavens and the Earth.
The Beauties and Ugly Spirits.
Thou design them all.

The Mighty Oceans are Happy.
The Rivers are Singing Allelujah.
While the Stars are Shinning.
The Trees Are Whispering.
The Flowers are Glowing and Singing for joy.

Power of all Powers.
Thou who holdest the Universe.
At the Palms of your hand.
You knows about Everything.
Oh! Mysterious One.
Thou art great indeed.

Collette Nlemchi. 2/2018.

12. THE GATES OF HEAVEN

Oh! Gates of Heaven forget me not.
Thou Mighty Gate.
You are like no other gate.
I praise you, thou gate of Perfection.
 Your Beauty and Design,
Is beyond human understanding.
You gate of Holliness.
Forget me not.
 Oh! Mighty Gate,
Bear me Witness,
I am doing the work of the Master,
And thou will open up for me,
As I enter into the Kingdom of Perfection.

 2/2018. Collette Nlemchi

13. ANGELS OF POWER

Powerful Angels of the King.
Thou are so Obedient and Happy.
Doing the work of the Master.
Thou Comet in different forms and Shape.
To protect and do the work of the Master.

Thou are scattered around the Globe fixing things all over.
Master is happy for you.
As you do his work on Earth.

You came in different forms and shapes.
For the Masters work you perform.
Thou shall obtain favor for the work you do.
For Master shall reward your Mission

Collette Nlemchi. 2018.

14. THE FOREST OF THE UNKNOWN

Deep at the Forest of The Unknown.
No Sign of Human Existence.
The Trees are Whispering.
The Birds are Humming.
>Here comes the Healing Herbs.
>Different kinds of Leaves.
>Waving their hands to be seen.
>The Tourists Found the leaves.
>The Herbs are all on the Ground.

Come on, Come on, they whisper.
We are the cure for your infirmities.
The Creator made us to Heal.
And we are here to Cure.
Cure You From all your Afflictions.

Collette Nlemchi.2/2018

15. TAKING AUTHORITY

Children of God, It is time to take Authority.
I take Authority over the Demons, Principalities.
And Spiritual Wickedness at High Places. IN JESUS NAME.
I take Authority over Sicknesses and Diseases.
I speak and come against fear, doubt, frustration,
And Spirit of Confusion IN JESUS NAME.
      I take Authority over Evil Forces of this World.
Against wicked Spirits, Cosmic Powers IN JESUS NAME.

Luke 9:1. And he called the Twelve Apostles Together.
And gave them power and Authority over all the Demons.
And to heal Diseases. Luke 10:19, Matthew 16:15-19.
Mathew 28:18, Mathew18:18-20,Romans 13:1, James 4:7.
Hebrews 13:17,1 John4:4,2Corinthians 10:3-5.

    Collette Nlemchi. 2018

16. UNDER YOUR UMBRELLA

Under your Umbrella I shall hide.
You have the greatest Amunition.
You are the greatest Daddy.
Thou art the biggest protector.
Under your Umbrella I shall hide.
I hide under your protection with my Family.

As the Wind blows we praise your name.
When the Sun shines, we honor you.
Under your Umbrella We shall hide.

Glory and Honor belongs to You.
Your Name Oh! Lord, shall be Glorified.
Even if Satan and His Agents are Horrified,
We will serve you all the days of our lives.

1-22-2018.Collette Nlemchi

17. LITTLE GOD/BIG GOD

They are the little gods.
They can do nothing.
They are the little gods.
They have no power.

I have a BIG GOD.
I Claim a BIG GOD.
He is Everything to me.
I have a Bigger GOD.
He can move my Mountains.

01/17/18. Collette Nlemchi

18. THOU THE UNFATHOMABLE SEA

Thou who healeth my infirmities.
From my Head to my Toes.
Thou hast healed me.
Thou who rewardest those who serve thee.
Master, do not let me Labor in Vain.
At Your Service, You art The Holy of Hollies.
Thou art the Unfathomable Sea.

2018. Collette Nlemchi

19. 7 DAYS OF PRAYER MANIFESTATION

- Oh! God of Heavens let the impossibilities in my life become possible IN JESUS NAME.
- I Cancel, I Destroy, and I Neutralize all Curses both known and Unknown IN JESUS NAME.
- Oh! God of Heavens make me to Succeed and bring me into Overflow IN JESUS NAME.
- I Command My Wicked Pursuers To Pursue themselves IN JESUS NAME.
- You my Devourers, Disappear from my labor IN JESUS NAME.
- Windows of Heaven Open Up For Me IN JESUS NAME.
- Let the Heaven and Earth come against all forces of darkness in my life IN JESUS NAME.
- I claim abundance in every area of my Life IN JESUS NAME.
- Oh! Ye my Breakthrough, begin to locate me IN JESUS NAME.
- Rain of Fire, What are you waiting For? I Command thee to Rain Fire on every Camp of the Enemies of My Breakthrough IN JESUS NAME.
- I Break and Command every Curse of Death From my home to Flee. IN JESUS NAME

I Command Thunder and Fire of God to break all strange meetings held against me IN JESUS NAME.

Failure to receive Miracles shall not be my portion IN JESUS NAME.

Collette Nlemchi. 10/31/09

20. GIVING THANKS TO THE KING OF KINGS

- Thou who created Heaven and Earth. I THANK YOU.
- Thou who made my impossibilities to become possible I THANK YOU.
- Thou who made the day and Night, I THANK YOU.
- For Your Protection, I THANK YOU.
- For my Family, I THANK YOU.
- For Being the greatest one, I THANK YOU.
- For my Destiny, I THANK YOU.
- For the Wealth You Giveth To do your Work, I THANK YOU.
- For Directing My Foot Steps. I THANK YOU.

Collette Nlemchi.

21. I GLORIFY YOUR NAME

- The Wonders of your Creation makes me to Wonder.
- Your Name is above all Names.
- You are the greatest one who gives and takes.
- Your Ways are not our Ways.
- Thou are full of Mysteries beyond human understanding.
- Have Mercy on me Oh! Mighty One.
- I am hiding under your Shadow.
- And thou protect me and my Family.
- And We shall serve you Forever.

4/22/18. Collette. Nlemchi

22. MYSTERIOUS ONE

There are Mysteries around us.
The Air we breath and the live you give.
You, the Unfathomable Sea.
Nothing, I say Nothing like thee.
Thou, Only Commands the Universe.
The Sun shines, while the Moon Laughs.
The Grasses and Trees are Whispering.
Here comes the Flowers, Singing for Joy.
Thou Only can understand their Tongues.

Collette Nlemchi

23. BEYOND HUMAN UNDERSTANDING

The Rivers are Flowing.
While the Damsels are Dancing.
Inside the Deepest Ocean.
Thou Findest different Creatures and Species.
These are Findings beyond Human Understanding.
All are Bowing Down For You.
For None, and None is like You.

Thou shall be praised from Generation to Generation.
Thou shall be honored because of your Creation.
How Wonderful, Powerful and Mighty Thou Art.

Collette Nlemchi.

24. IS ALL ABOUT YOU

The World is all about You.
Thou who giveth and taketh.
You Created Heaven and Earth.
You have all the Powers on Earth.
The Raindrops Testify your Glory.
And The THUNDER hammers on Evil.

Never did you forsake the Righteous.
Miraculously, you opened up the door.
And there is breakthrough.
The Red Sea Becomes Open.
Pharoah and his Hench Men were Drowned.
This shows, you are Power of all Powers.
And None shall withstand Your Wrath.

   Collette Nlemchi. 10/7/2018

25. UNIVERSE

Oh! Universe forget not the Love I give
As I give love to Universe So shall I receive
As I offer Prayers, So I shall receive.
Mistake me not.
This is not about Crazy Love
It is 100% Spiritual and pure Love
As I am an Angel to the Needy
I have Zeallions of Cherubis that work with me

Oh! Universe, thou shall provide for me that which I need
I am doing the work of JAH
Thou shall supply my needs
I will not give up until I accomplish my mission
To serve you is my greatest Joy
I am a servant to the Greatest
I bow down and serve the Highest
Unspeakable Joy I shall have.

Collette Nlemchi. 07/20/2010

26. WORRY NOT

Worry Not Lament Not. About What?
That which you do not have any control.
He sees everything under the Sun.
He is the greatest One.
And he shall replace Loses.
Because, there is always a reason for everything.

He designet the Kingdom for his betterment.
He has the power to quench the Anomalies.
His ways are not our ways.
The way we see things are different.
What you condemn is that which he cherish.

Weep not for the Comforter has filled your Worries.
Thou regain all you have lost.
And in a twinkle of an eye.
Thou shall see the Light.
Light shall not depart from thee.
Because of thy Goodness and Righteousness.

Collette Nlemchi. 10/7/2018

27. ANGELS OF GOODWILL

Oh! Yee Mysterious Creatures.
Standing by my Side.
Thou art Fighting Mysterious Battle.
To Protect the Chosen Ones.
The Righteous Shall Win The Battle.
In this World of Imperfection.

Heaven and Earth Adore Thee.
Seas and Oceans are Singing Alleluyah.
While the Rivers are Flowing with Joy.
Thy Protection is Highly Needed.
And we thy Chosen Ones shall Everlasting serve thee.
No greater Joy to be chosen and that is the greatest gift of all.
And unto thy Kingdom We shall Dwell, Everlasting and Everlasting.

Collette Nlemchi. 10/7/2018.

28. I WILL ALWAYS PRAISE THEE

Oh! Heaven, thou shall always be praised by me.
Your Chosen Ones Honors and Adore thee.
Thou art the greatest of all.
On Your Throne, I shall dwell.
No Happiness Greater than this.
Thou shall make perfect my Foot steps.
The way I thinket and Doet.
Thou shall perfect my ways.
And I shall not fall inside a Pit.
Thou shall provide me with Cherubis to prevent me from Falling.
Holy and Glorious are thou, Thou Restoreth thy Kingdom.

Collette Nlemchi. 10/7/2018

29. THE WICKED SHALL PERISH

Put no Trust in Evil Spirits.
Put no trust in Principalities.
These are the Wicked Spirits.
Unto Hail Fire they shall Burn.
They oppress Humanity and no Conscience for their Wickedness.
They are trying to stop the work of Glory.
And Heaven is Telling them "I AM THAT I AM".

No Power ever lived shall withstand your Wrath.
Thou shall strike and destroy their Existence.
Thou who is the Author of Redemption, and the giver of Perfection.
GLORY, GLORY, GLORY, UNTO YOU.

Collette Nlemchi. 10/7/2018

30. WORD OF KNOWLEDGE

Oh! Heavenly Father, I adore Cherish and Worship You.

Thou who Created Heaven and Earth, I worship You.

John 3:16. For God so loved the World and gave his only Son.

That whosoever believe in him shall not perish but have Eternal Life.

Brethren, we should learn to forgive as Jesus have taught us to do.

Inherit Eternal Life. Try to forgive those who have wronged you and have.

The battle for God to fight. The KING OF KINGS and the Lord of Lords is the Greatest Warrior.

There is no Battle that he cannot Fight. Why not Relax and let him take care of Business against your.

Enemies. You should not forget the special Prayers which he taught us to pray. Matthew 6:9-13.

Pray then like this 'Our Father, who art in Heaven, Hallow be thy name, thy Kingdom come, your will be.

Done on Earth as it is in Heaven. Give us this day our daily Bread, and forgive us our Sins as we forgive.

Those who Trespass against us and lead us not into Temptation, but deliver us from all evil Amen.'

Remember, when you are under his Umbrella, You are chosen and a Kingdom Person art thou.

Therefore, No Evil, shall befall thee and he will dispatch his Powerful Angels to fight for you.

*Remember, do the work of God with your whole heart not just lip Service. Do not be Hypocritical to his

Service. Serve him with your whole Heart because not every one that calls Lord, Lord will enter his.

Kingdom but he that does the will of the Father. Matthew 7:21-23.

*Mess not with my Anointed Ones and to my Prophets do no Harm. The Lord is talking about his real.

Chosen Ones and not Fake Prophets or Sorcerers. Ps 105:15. * Be Careful how you mess with God's.

Anointed Ones because the Wrath of God shall befall you.

I Respect and honor anything that is of God, and anything not of God I Dishonor.. C.N. *However, if the.

So called Chosen Ones turns to Wickedness, They will be banished from the Kingdom of God.*However, there Is always room for Repentance if they choose.*

*The Chosen Ones are under the Shadow of the Almighty God, that means they are highly protected and.

If any Demon come to attack them, the Master will Strike with his Powerful Angels*. CN. Children of God if.

You Serve The Greatest One, He will Answer.

*For Example, Your Children, if somebody, comes to attack them, what are you going to do? Are you

Going to stay there and say, it is OK. I Know You. You will use everything Humanly and Spiritually possible

to fight back. Some of you will use Gun, Stones, Hammer to attack the Attacker. This is the way we are to

our Heavenly Father, He Fights the Battle for us. We are protected as Kingdom People and he will

dispatch his Dangerous and Powerful Angels To Fight For us. Based on this Analogy, when you serve God

be assured that your Battle will be fought In Jesus Name.*

Collette Nlemchi. 10/9/18

31. DARKNESS SHALL FOLLOW ITS OWN IN JESUS NAME

*Rejoice Oh! Righteous One, Be of good Faith. Perfection shall Reward Thee.

You Mobile Darkness Pursuing My Destiny, Thou must Die In Jesus Name.

*Every Load of Darkness Programmed against my Life shall Scatter In Jesus Name.

*All Darkness Hovering Around Me Must Dissolve IN JESUS NAME.

*Arrows of Darkness Fired Unto My Star, Backfire In Jesus Name.

*Arrows of Darkness fired unto my Head Back Fire In Jesus Name.

*Satanic Agents of Dark Weapons Die Now and Kill Yourself In Jesus Name.

The God of 1 Minute Miracle, 24hrs Miracle, 36hrs Miracle, 48hrs Miracles, 96 Hours Miracles Everlasting Time Miracles.. Thou Shall Locate Me In Jesus Name.

Collette Nlemchi.10/17/2018

32. CARNAL MINDED AND SPIRITUAL MINDED

Brethren a lot of you are carnal Minded. Let us look at Romans 8.

V6. To be Carnally Minded is Death, but Spiritually Minded is Life and Peace.

V7. Carnal Mind is Enmity against God. It is not subject to the Will of God.

V8. Therefore, If you are in Flesh, You cannot please God.

HOLD UNTO THE SCRIPTURES

JOHN 14:V.1. If you shall ask anything in my Name, I shall do.

Hosea 4:6. My People are destroyed because of lack of Knowledge.

MATTHEW 18:10. Take heed that ye despise not these little ones, for I say unto you. That in heaven their Angels do always behold the Face Of my Father which is in Heaven.

ISAIAH 49:25. I will Contend with them that Contend with Thee and I will save thy Children.

33. PRAYERS TO MAKE STRAIGHT MY CROOKED PARTS

Oh! Supernatural and Invisible Father.
I come To You At This Hour Of The Day.
Make Thou My Life Straight.
I seek Only You and No Other.
Because In You There Is Light.

I have gone through the Valley Of Life.
Heaven Knows There is None Like You.
Thou are the Only One That Knows The Answer.
The Keys To Heaven and Earth Belongs To You.
And To Whom You Give, there comes Eternal Life.

In thy Hands are changeable Times.
In a Twinkle of an Eye thou Changest Things.
All Impossibilities becomes Possible.
Sickness, Diseases, Backwardness are destroyed.
And all Curses goes back to the Senders.
Thou has lightened up my ways and crooked Parts Thou maket straight.

Collette Nlemchi. 02/06/10

34. VOICES OF THE ANGELS

I heard the Voice of The Angels.
While I was doing The Work Of Light.
They Shouted Alleluia, Alleluia,
Her Destiny is being Fulfilled.
Oh! Heaven, I thank you for Restoration.

Demon Spirits and Workers of Iniquities are Chastised.
Their Powers On Earth are Chastised and Paralyzed.
The Light Have Lifted Me Up From The Pits Of This World.
I will Flourish And Prosper In The Land.

Oh! Light, None Like thee in this World We Live.
You that does The Impossible.
You that heal the Sick and Blind Eyes You Open.
All The Infirmities In My Body You Heal.
Mighty and Everlasting Father.
All Power and Praises belong To You.

Collette Nlemchi. 2010

35. POWER AND HOPE

In you I have found Power and Hope.
There is No Other That Giveth Life and Hope.
With You By My Side, I claim a Breakthrough.
All Impossibilities are Made Possible.
And all Crookedness in my Life is Straight.

The Omnipotent, Powerful and Supernatural Deity.
I have come to your Throne.
And all My Blessings shall be Permanent.
The Doors You have Opened shall not be closed.
I Paralyze and Cripple All Forces That are Trying To Close The
Divine Doors.

Collette Nlemchi. 2010.

36. NATURE THOU ART GOOD

Oh! Nature, Favor me because am good to you.
I appreciate the Birds that Fly.
The Invisible Wind, how I Love You.
Trees and Grasses Blossom For Joy.
Roses and Lillies Of The Valley, where are You?

The Trees at The Orchard makes Me To Wonder.
Rivers and The Ocean Flows For Joy.
During Famine, Nature Feeds It's Subjects.
Oh! Nature, How Wonderful art Thou?
You made the birds of the air.
The Mountains, Rivers And The Ocean.
All Are Happy For Thee.

Collette Nlemchi 2010.

37. MISSION ACCOMPLISHED

Your Direction, Oh! Lord, I shall follow.
That is the Highway To Happiness.
Your Road Map Guides my Ways.
It also guide me To The Streets Of Gold.
Human Roads Are Made With Highways and Cities.
Your Highway Oh! Lord is Made with Patience and Prayers.

With Prayers, and Patience, I shall reach my Destination.
Be Obedient To God's Direction.
And That Will Take You To The Right Destination.
Right Destination, Takes You To Mission Accomplished.

Collette Nlemchi. 2010

38. MIGHTY GOD

You are a mighty God.
One Who Destroys The Heads Of Dragons.
All Over the World, Thou art Praised.
For Thou has Paralyzed The Work Of Demons.

Thou show me Good Dreams.
Bad Dreams, thou have Cancelled.
Thou Have Cancelled Generational Curses.
Unto Your Chosen Vessels, Comes Generational Blessings.

Collette Nlemchi. 2010.

39. GENERATIONAL BLESSINGS

Your Kindness cannot be compared.
Your Compassion Touches My Heart.
Your Miracles are Beyond Human Understanding.
Holy One, You are All I know.

Your gentleness is all I want.
Your Holliness makes me To Wonder.
Your Protection is What I Need.
You Will Guide in Everything I do.

I thank you for destroying generational Curses.
I thank you for my Generational Blessings.
I thank You For Restoring My Losses.
Your Greatness is all I want.

Collette Nlemchi. 2/21/2011

40. PRAYER FOR PROTECTION AGAINST ENEMIES

Oh! Powerful, Wonderful and Universal Commander.
All Powers Both on Earth and In Heaven Belongs To You.
You have Dominion Over all Forces of Darkness.
Your Powers and Wonders Cannot Be Explained.
You Know The Known and The Unknown.
Thou also Holdest The Key To defend your Subjects In This Universe.

With Your Command, all my Enemies are Destroyed.
It is only You who fight this Battle For us..
I put all these Attackers and Enemies in your hands.
And Thou Shall Strike To Protect These Thy Chosen Ones.

Collette Nlemchi. 2011

41. INVOKING YOUR ANGELS

Oh! Servants of the most High God.
Messengers of Peace and Great Warriors.
I am calling you to come from all walks of life.
To protect my Rights.
Send us messages of good Will.
At Last We shall Glorify Our Lord.

Collette Nlemchi. 2011

42. MYSTRIES AROUND US

I have a Story To Tell You.
It is a Story About This Life.
This Life is Full Of Mysteries.
There are different Kinds of Spirits.
They are Flying around the Globe.
They come in different Colors,
Forms, Sizes, to the confusion of Mankind.

Some of them are divine workers doing the work of God.
Some are Bad Spirits Stopping The Affairs of Mankind.
Here Comes the Angels Rolling The Stones Away.
They are Carrying The Cross Doing The Work Of Jah.

Collette Nlemchi. 2018

43. MY GREATNESS

Oh! Ye my Greatness.
Thou shall not be limited.
Thou shall fulfill thy Destiny.
Given to you by Heaven Highest.
Thou the Author and Speaker of Revelation.
With thy Power, thou shall crush Destiny Killers.
Thou shall send your powerful sages to destroy them all.

My greatness, thou shall not give up.
Keep trying and you will reach the Top.
I see you at the top and your Enemies Foot Stool.
The Light has put you at the Top.
Be grateful because it is not by thy power.

Oh! Power of Powers, we honor and thank thee.
For that which you did.
You turneth Impossibility to Possibility.
Only you have all the Powers.
Shalom, Shalom, Oh! Master.

Collette Nlemchi. 10/17/2018

44. MAGIC MIRACLE WORDS (SAY IT 10 TIMES)

Thou shall supply all my needs.
According to your Riches (PHILIPPIANS 4:19).
My Enemies are Powerless.
And are my Footstool.

Collette Nlemchi. 12/2/2018

45. LIGHT SURPASSES DARKNESS

In you there comes Light.
You light up the Heavens.
With unquenchable Light.
Light that is immaculate and Brilliant.
You put Light where there is Darkness.

Collette Nlemchi. 12/2/2018

46. MY ANCESTORS

Where are you my Ancestors?
I can feel the pain and Agony.
Thou Tillest the Ground with Sweat.
History shall not forget you.
Some of you carried the cross of life.
While some of you were disgusting and Brutal to the end.
Some are also busy stalking and monitoring people.
Some are Road Blockers, Enemies of Progress.

Did you do the work of life?
Were you busy Brutalizing People?
Some of you did Extraordinary Things,
Which is beyond Human understanding.
Some climbed the highest Mountain.
Some performed Supernatural Miracles.
Where are You? Did you make it? Up there?
Or are you at the Ugly Side?

Collette Nlemchi. 12/2/18

47. KINGDOM OF THE BLESSED

OH! Kingdom of the Blessed.
How I behold you.
I shall someday Embrace thee.
Where there is Joy Unspeakable.
No Evil Creatures Dwelleth Around Thee.
Kingdom full of grace and Glory.

The Raindrops Testify.
How I adore thee.
How Wonderful thou art.
For thy perfection I Magnify.
Holy and Great thou Art.

    Collette Nlemchi. 11/1/2018

48. SPIRITUAL DARKNESS ARRESTED

All forces of darkness working against the work of God,
You are all arrested because of Wickedness.
Thou who created the World, thou art still in Control of the Universe.

Thou shall send your Cherubis.
From all Four Corners of the WORLD.
To stop these hindering spirits.
Working against my destiny.
Oh! Heaven thou has paralyzed.
and demolished them all.

The wealth you gave them, they doet not the work of God.
They are busy trying to stop the order and command of the Kingdom.
Unto Hail Fire they shall burn.
And at the end, they shall not enter the Kingdom of the Blessed.

Collette Nlemchi. 11/2/2018

49. ENEMIES OF MY CALLING ATTACKED

Attacking the Enemies of my Destiny.

*The Lord has overcome the world. We must attack the enemies of our calling IJN. John 16:37.

*I sharpen my Spiritual Sword against the enemies of my calling In Jesus Name.

*Matt.16:18—And the Lord said unto thee, that thou art Peter and upon this Rock I will build my Church and the gates of hell shall not prevail against it.

*Every spiritual defilement in my life shall be cleansed by the Mighty Blood of Jesus. Amen.

*Any Satanic Hold, delay in my life shall be destroyed by the Mighty Power of God In Jesus Name.

50. LIFT UP OUR GOD

Our God Created Heaven and Earth.
Our God is a Wonderful God.
Our God is Powerful.
Our God is Omnipotent.
Our God is Everlasting.
Our God is the Best.
Our God is the Greatest.
Our God Is Powerful.
Our God is Miraculous.
Our God is the Commander in Chief.
Our God Has the Greatest Amunition.
None is like Our God.
Our God is Endless.
And Endless is his Name.
He has No Beginning.
And He has no End.
Wonderful, Beyond Human Understanding.

Collette Nlemchi. 8/6/19

Printed in the United States
By Bookmasters